"We have more possibilities available in each moment than we realise."

-Thich Nhat Hanh

How to Drink a Glass of Water

A publication from The Right-brain Workout.

First published by The Right-brain Workout, in 2023.

Text copyright © Alex Wadelton, 2023.

The moral right of the author has been asserted.

All rights reserved. No part of this book may be reproduced, stored in a retrieval system, or transmitted in any form or by any means, electronic, mechanical, photocopying, recording, or otherwise, without the prior written permission of the copyright holder.

Designed and Illustrated by Damian Galvin.
Unauthorised reproduction of any part of this book's design or illustrations is strictly prohibited.

For inquiries, please contact The Right-brain Workout
alex@rightbrainworkout.com or visit our website at
rightbrainworkout.com

The information provided in this book is for educational and entertainment purposes only. The author and publisher are not responsible for any actions or decisions made by readers based on the content of this book. Please consult with a medical professional or relevant experts for any health-related concerns.

All product names, trademarks, and registered trademarks mentioned in this book are the property of their respective owners. Use of these names does not imply endorsement.

Contents

Chapter 1. Selecting a glass for your water.......19

Chapter 2. Picking up your glass.........................23

Chapter 3. Pouring your glass of water..............27

Chapter 4. Looking at your glass of water.........31

Chapter 5. Thanking everyone who made your glass of water possible..............35

Chapter 6. The journey of your water.................39

Chapter 7. Taking your first sip of water............43

Chapter 8. Listening to your water......................49

Chapter 9. The water's endless journey..............53

Chapter 10. Your glass of water is infinite...........59

Chapter 11. Finishing your glass of water...........63

Foreword

The wellness world is full of wankery.

This book thankfully cuts through the wank and lets you appreciate the simple things in life and just how beautiful the world around us really is.

Who knew so much joy could be found in simply drinking a glass of water.

- Tommy Little

Author's Note

I came up for the idea for this simple book, when on a flight from Sydney to Melbourne.

Usually, I love sitting in the window seat so I can stare at the incredible beauty of the clouds and marvel at the fact that I am flying through the air at more then eight-hundred kilometres an hour, thousands of metres above the ground.

It's a sight that the greatest minds in history, like Leonardo da Vinci, Joan of Arc, Nikola Tesla, Cleopatra, Montezuma and anyone born before the advent of flight would have been absolutely dazzled by.

On this occasion, however, I was sat in the middle seat.

As the plane lifted off the ground, I comforted myself with the thought that at least I'd be able to glimpse over the shoulder of the woman seated next to me, at the passing clouds.

However as soon as I thought that, she closed the window cover, put her headphones in, and started watching a Netflix show on her mobile.

The re-boot of The Addams Family, "Wednesday" it was. It's a very good show, but not a patch on the miracle of flight, in my opinion.

So, I decided to do something else.

I decided to ask for a glass of water from the flight attendant, and enjoy that water for as long as the rest of the flight went for.

The next thirty minutes or so was one of the most profound moments of my life.

I thought about many things I'd only given a cursory thought to before.

My mind travelled through the entire history of our planet and the infinite future of the Universe.

And beyond.

That is what this book is about.

I hope you enjoy it as much as I enjoyed that glass of water.

The entire history of our planet and the infinite future of the Universe.

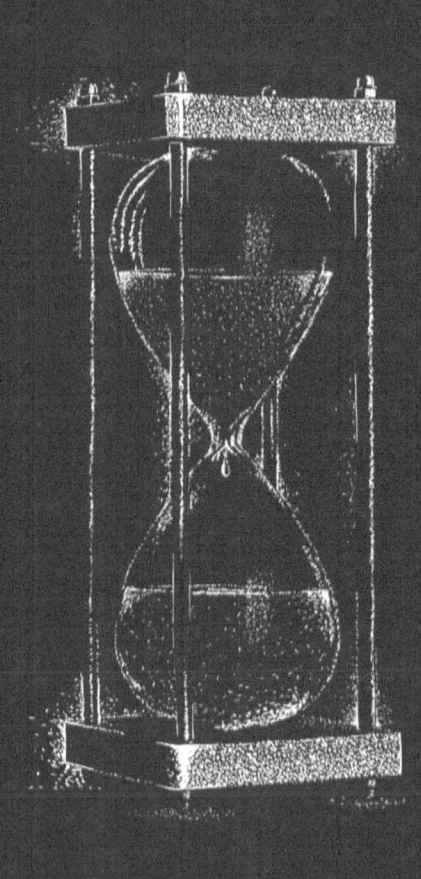

Preface

Much of modern life is a real hurry.

We wake up and hurry to have a coffee to wake us up more.

We hurry to get breakfast ready.

We hurry out the door to get to work, get to school, or get to wherever it is we are rushing to.

We get stuck in traffic jams on the way to work, getting frustrated, and arriving late and harried.

We look at our phone as we busy ourselves.

We work over lunch, working on our computer as we spoon food into our mouth.

We stare at the telly as we eat dinner.

We are distracted by screens, and their constant need to be fed attention.

Life is busy.

So very busy.

It feels like there aren't enough hours in the day.

But there is another way.

A slower way.

A more mindful way.

A way that anyone can do.

With no training. No life hacks. And no celebrity endorsement.

It's the simplest thing in the world.

S l o w.

D o w n.

A beautiful way to slow down is to set aside thirty minutes, once a week, to drink a glass of water.

You can find once a week to spend thirty minutes drinking a glass of water, can't you?

Usually when we drink a glass of water, we don't really think about it.

We are thirsty, so we drink a glass of water.

We are hot, so we drink a glass of water.

Our mouth is dry, so we drink a glass of water.

But when you slow down and think about drinking your glass of water, you can make the first step to a fulfilling life.

A life lived in the present moment.

A life open to love.

A life open to the beauty and magic of the every day moment.

A life connected to every single creature on the planet.

Through all of past history, and all of the infinite future.

Yes, all of that is contained in one glass of water!

You see, when you drink a glass of water, you are drinking in something with an incredible story.

Something that contains the mysteries of the universe.

So, let's learn the art of drinking a glass of water.

Together.

By the end, the glass will be empty.

But your cup will be full.

So, let's learn the art of drinking a glass of water.

Chapter One

Selecting a glass for your water

Before you can drink a glass of water, you need to have a glass to put the water into.

There are almost limitless options when it comes to selecting a glass to drink water from.

You may have a tall glass, or an old coffee mug, or you may even decide to drink from an old jam jar.

Whichever you choose, before you pick it up, look at it... and think about how the glass you hold is the result of thousands upon thousands of years of human ingenuity.

Because when you start to think deeply about your glass, you begin to understand that millions of years ago, the notion of a "glass" did not even exist.

Water was drunk by animals sipping from a lake or river.

Perhaps a plant hydrated itself after a refreshing rain fall.

When humans began to walk the lands, they first began to cup their hands to catch falling rain, or splash water flowing through a river.

What a miracle it is for you to be able to reach onto a shelf and select a glass, a mug, or a jam jar!

Hundreds of years ago, glasses were handcrafted by artisans with many years of training.

It was a laborious, hot, and dangerous process to make something so beautiful and delicate.

Back then, glasses were the domain of the wealthy, as the poor had to make do with a cup made out of wood or metal or clay.

And now, here you stand in the kitchen, perhaps with many glasses to choose from.

A glass made by the million inside a factory, thousands of miles from where you live, where robots work twenty four hours a day producing perfect glass after perfect glass after perfect glass.

A glass that's travelled around the world.

A glass touched by dozens of people along the way before you purchased it in a store.

Think of the lives of all of the people who made it possible for you to drink from the glass.

You see, even selecting a glass to drink from can be a beautiful few moments of quiet reflection, a glimpse back into the history of humankind, and a wondrous time for gratitude for this most basic of utensils.

Now, you are ready to pick up your glass.

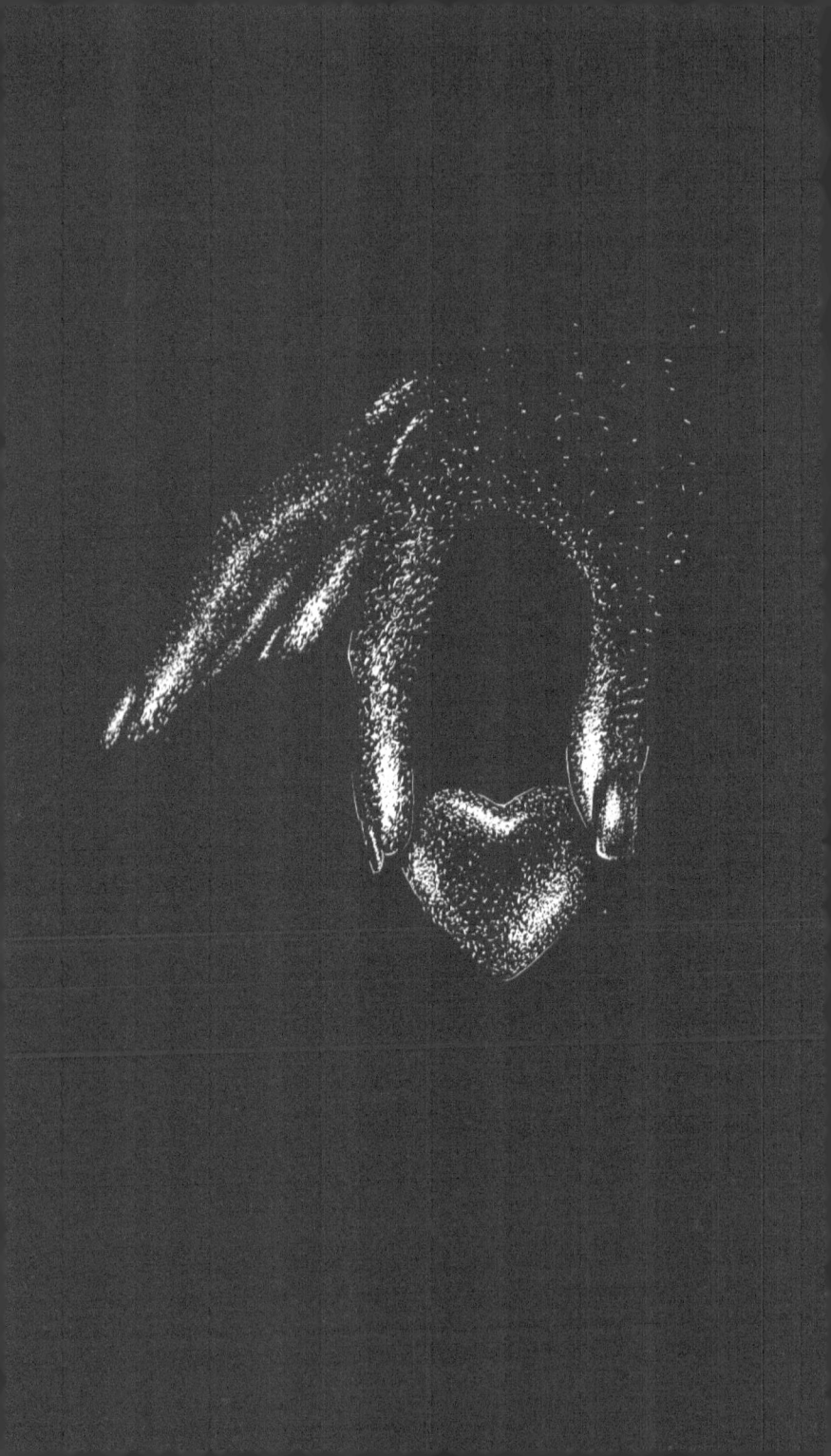

Chapter Two

Picking up your glass

It seems so simple.

Just pick up the glass.

But, you should try to think about picking up the glass.

Because you will feel the cool touch of the glass against your fingers.

If you concentrate, you will even feel your heart beat pulsing through your fingers against the glass.

A heart beat that powers your body without you ever having to think about it.

A heart beat that pushes blood around your entire body.

A heart that's beating inside every single human being right at this very moment.

Thump, thump, thump.

I am alive. I am alive. I am alive.

From your birth, until your death.

Eight billion people with this incredible organ that sustains life on this planet right now.

Billions of years of evolution that enable you to be standing or sitting here reflecting on the joy of being able to drink a glass of water.

Then, think of all of the people from the past who had this miraculous heart in their chest.

Then, the billions and billions, if not trillions of creatures that roam this planet who also have a heart beating away inside of them.

We are all connected in this way.

You can unravel the sheer enormity of the universe just by feeling the pulse of your heart in your fingers against the side of the glass.

Now, you are ready to put the water into your glass.

You can unravel the sheer enormity of the universe just by feeling the pulse of your heart in your fingers against the side of the glass.

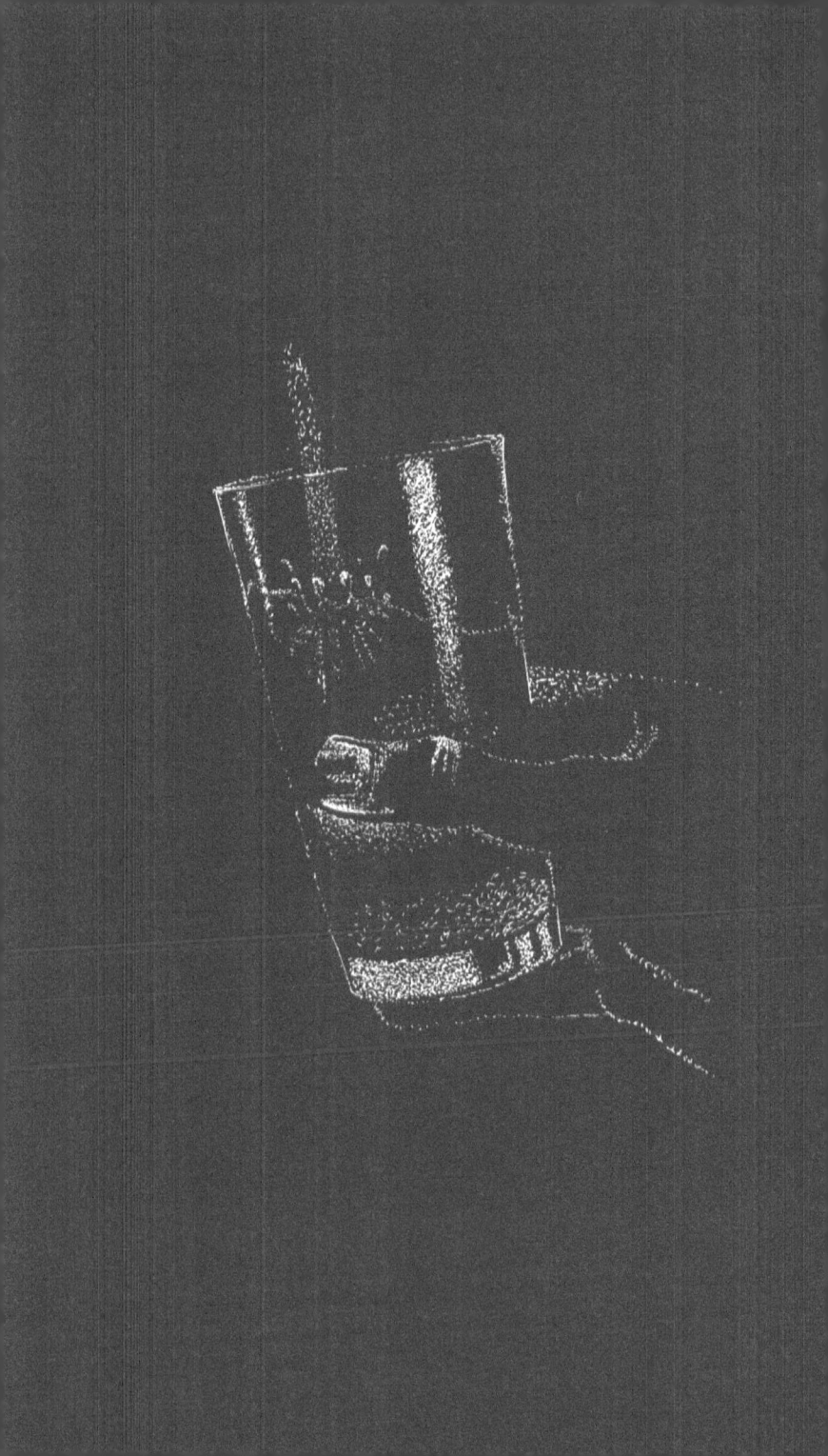

Chapter Three

Pouring your glass of water

Many of you will have a bottle of water to pour your water from.

Others may be pouring the water from a jug.

Or perhaps from a tap.

Whichever way you choose to fill your glass up, you can think about where that utensil has come from.

How did the water bottle come into your possession?

What materials has gone into making the jug?

How incredible is it to turn a tap and for water to pour effortlessly into your glass?

As the water begins to fall, you can see the light glistening. Perhaps it may be reflecting your surroundings too.

You can easily tune into the sounds that are being made as the water cascades and then hits the bottom of your glass.

Watch as it swirls around, leaping up, settling down, ever filling up towards the brim of the glass.

It truly is a quite wonderful ceremony to be a part of, if you concentrate on the right now of your being.

You can watch bubbles form, get larger, and then pop away, never to exist again.

A whole life lived in just fractions of a second.

Some might say that your life too could be likened to that of a bubble in a glass of water.

You are formed, you grow up, and then you are gone, transformed into another form.

What do you make of your time here?

When you glass is full, you can move on to looking at your glass of water.

You are formed, you grow up, and then you are gone, transformed into another form.

Chapter Four

Looking at your glass of water

Water is a magical conductor of sound.

Do you remember that scene in the movie Jurassic Park, when the Tyrannosaurus Rex is approaching?

We see a glass of water vibrating with every step of the dinosaur, the circular ripples floating outwards.

You can experiment with this by drumming your fingers on the surface to the side of your glass of water.

Or you can hit the table upon where the glass sits. Watch as different ripples form.

You can pick up the glass and swirl it around slowly and watch as the water moves up the inside of the glass.

Perhaps you'd like to hold the glass up above your eye-line and look up and through the bottom of the glass?

The surroundings will be stretched and distorted depending on the shape of your glass and what is around you.

You'll see yourself in the water, and you can think where do I start, where does the glass start, and where does the water start?

Depending on where your water is from, the chemical analysis of it may be slightly different.

Your glass of water may have more minerals in it than someone else's. Or less.

But, isn't it incredible that you can't see any of it? It's all hidden from view but it's there.

So too it is with people. We only can see what is in front of our eyes, but what lies beneath is infinitely more complex and unfathomable in its own way.

What beauty lies within!

And you still have not taken a sip!

We only can see what is in front of our eyes, but what lies beneath is infinitely more complex and unfathomable in its own way.

Chapter Five

Thanking everyone who made your glass of water possible

The last part of the journey of this water to you, and your glass, has been facilitated by a wide array of humans.

If the water has come from a tap, think of all of the pipes, all of the planning, and all of the work required to install the plumbing underneath the earth to deliver the water to your house.

These facilities have been developed, tweaked, and improved over generations.

The ancient Romans set up aqueducts that enabled them to have running water in their homes thousands of years ago.

Yet, over time, these technological advancements were lost in the dusts of time.

How delicate is human knowledge, that ideas that were once ubiquitous can disappear, causing us to have to restart the process of invention once more?

All the while, the other inhabitants of the Earth, the flora and fauna, kept the same relationship with water that they developed over millions of years.

Only us humans have advanced our thinking beyond pure survival into the mastery of the elements.

And this has been made possible by generation after generation of humans working together to improve the delivery of fresh, clean drinking water that flows out of a tap at the flick of a hand.

Isn't it incredible to be a part of a lineage that is only a few thousand years old, that has seen us move from the invention of the wheel, to flying to planets millions upon millions of kilometres away?

How lucky you are to be living in a country where such clean water is taken for granted.

Many parts of the world are still dealing with polluted water. Water that has to be carried by foot to their starving families in terrible conditions.

It's the least we can do to honour how blessed we are to have such water freely available.

By slowing down, and taking the time to truly drink a glass of water, you can pay respects to the millions of people who don't have the luxury to be able to neglect the beauty of a glass of water.

When you have done so, you are ready for the next step in the enjoyment of your glass of water.

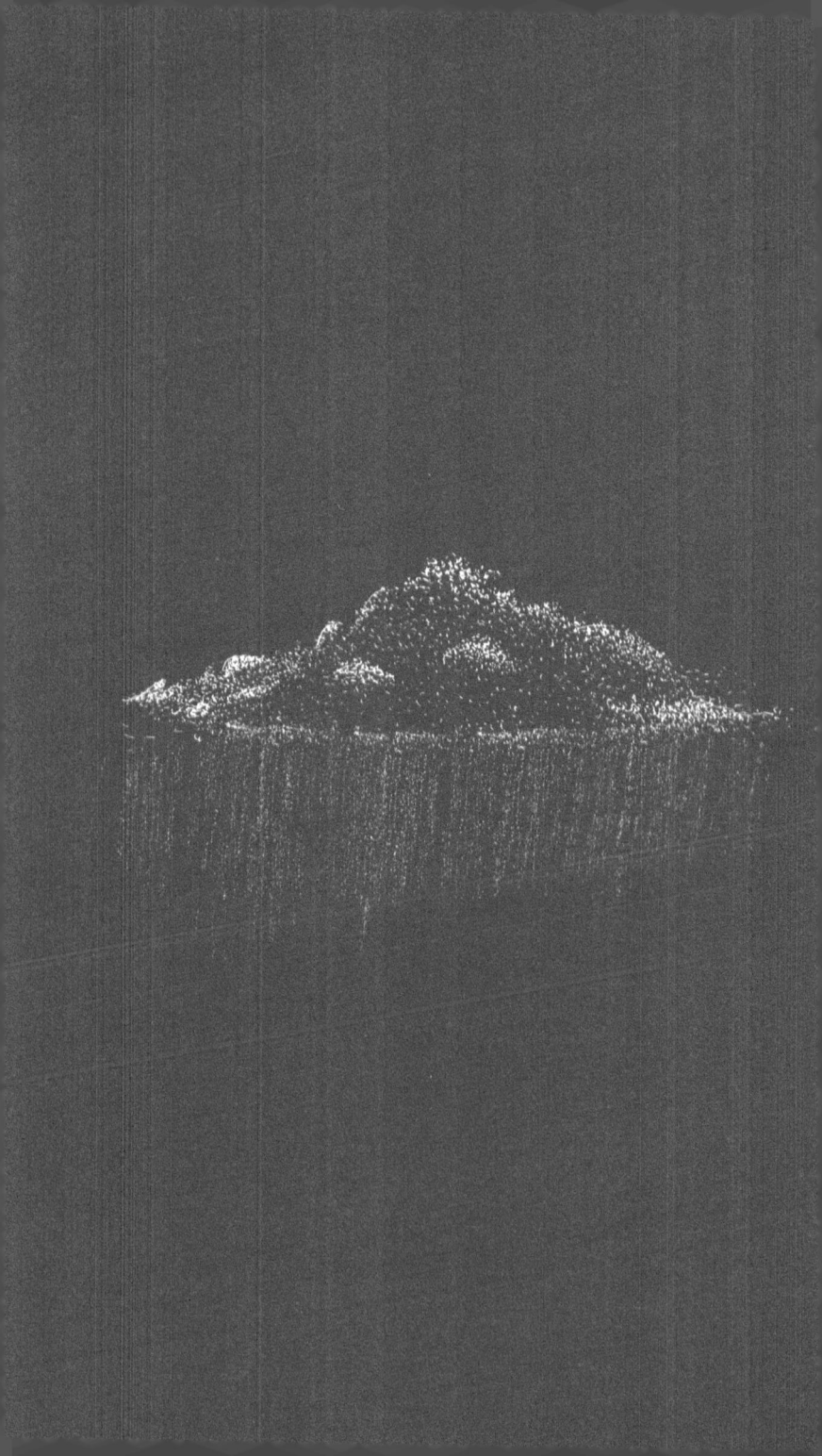

Chapter Six

The journey of your water

Your glass is full of water.

Now, you can start to think about the water itself.

We are all aware of the chemical make-up of the water, H_2O: two parts hydrogen to one part oxygen.

And that's before we even factor in its epic journey before human intervention.

Have you ever been flying in a plane on a cloudy day, looking at the ever-stretching horizon?

It's an awe-inspiring sight to see these clouds blanketing the Earth.

From this distance, if you didn't know, you'd think the clouds were solid objects, not unlike wool or cotton.

But as you sit there, inside this huge mechanical plane travelling at eight hundred kilometres per hour, containing hundreds of other people, you can fly straight through without a scratch!

Your eyes can deceive you. For what you thought you know and what you learn, can often be at opposite ends of the spectrum.

From these clouds, the water falls through the air.

This rain may fall on a city, a forest, a mountain, or into a lake.

It trickles down with gravity, being filtered by rocks, being sipped on by animals, swam through by fish, and helping crops grow.

Yet at the same time, water can cause floods, erode coastlines, and turn giant cliffs into sandy beaches.

The Yin-Yang nature of much of the world is what makes being alive such a beautiful experience.

The water in your glass has travelled from the clouds.

But what of its travels before that?

What forms has it taken?

As water it will have been drank by animals, helped plants grow, fallen as snow, turned into ice, and been part of an iceberg.

It may have witnessed an ancient apocalypse that wiped out the dinosaurs.

It may have existed when the Renaissance artists were creating beauty.

And when the first humans rose onto two feet, your water may have sustained life.

But beyond being "water" it's been much more than that.

Consider that a human, such as you, is seventy-five per cent water.

Therefore, does it not stand to reason that at some stage over the last few billion years, the water in your glass may have been a key building block of a huge range of living beings?

Humans, for sure. Perhaps the Woolly Mammoth. Or a frog. A tiny insect. A slug. Mega fauna. Tiny fish. Giant fish. Everything, and anything, everywhere.

And, now, here it is. Sitting in a glass. Awaiting your first sip.

What a journey. What a miracle!

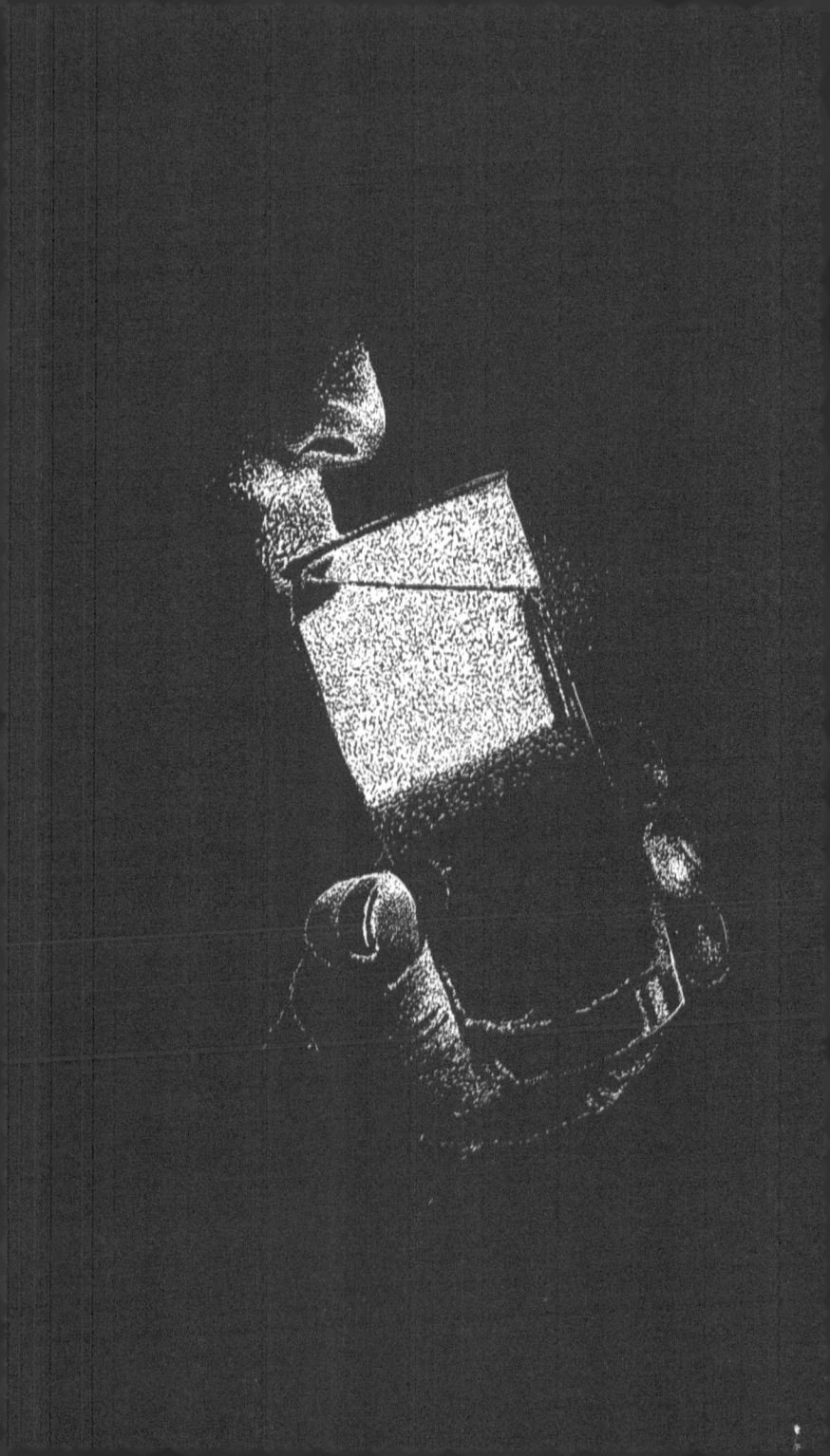

Chapter Seven

Taking your first sip of water

Already you have experienced so much more than a drink with this glass of water.

Gratitude.

Contemplation.

Beauty.

When you do such things, you can almost shake your head at the sheer amount of energy, life, and magic inside just this one glass.

The universe is inside each droplet of this water.

And this glass contains millions upon millions of droplets, all together, all as one.

So, it's only right that you smile at your water.

It has brought you so much joy already just by being in front of you now.

So, now, use both hands to bring the water to your lips.

Breathe it in. Smile at it. Savour the beautiful transparency of this liquid.

As you put the glass to the lips, you can feel the coolness of the glass.

As you gently tip the glass up, the water hits your lips, and then your teeth.

Feel it. Savour it. It has taken so much to get to you today.

It is such a beautiful moment to be in right now.

All that matters is the here and the now.

These are not new words to ponder, but they are words we all too often neglect.

That is the magic of drinking a glass of water.

It is a bell of mindfulness to be present and to realise that every breath is a miracle.

The water on your tongue, and in your mouth, can be moved so easily with the contraction of a few muscles in the face. A face that is itself a miracle of evolution.

How often do you think about the muscles in your face?

They can help you communicate feelings of happiness, sadness, disgust, fear, anger, and surprise.

They help you eat and drink.

Help you talk.

Whistle.

Blink.

These facial muscles are with you everyday, and they are present to help you enjoy your first sip of water.

Billions of years ago, the only creatures on this planet were single cell organisms, and now you can do everything you do every day with hardly a conscious thought.

You can walk, jump, and run. You can write a letter to a dear friend. You can drive a car to a mountaintop. You can do countless beautiful things with unconscious perfection.

That is why being conscious of drinking a glass of water can bring you back to who you truly are.

And the first swallow of this liquid? How beautiful it is.

You have many more mouthfuls of water to enjoy.

Take

Your.

Time.

For this glass of water is everything.

Being conscious of drinking a glass of water can bring you back to who you truly are.

Chapter Eight

Listening to your water

We don't often contemplate the noise that a sip of water can generate.

So, as you continue the slow and considered drinking of your glass of water perhaps you may use your mouth to make it sing.

With your lips pursed, you can whistle with it, creating a kind of birdsong.

The beautiful tweet of a far away bird is with you as you drink your glass of water.

By pushing the liquid around your mouth you can create a drum beat of sorts as the water ricochets across the inside of your cheek, thumps against your tongue, and squeezes through the gaps in your teeth.

And then you swallow.

A deep guttural sound in your throat forces the water down inside of you, to begin its remarkable journey around your body.

This liquid has now transmitted sounds for your ears to drink in.

In a way, you are drinking your glass of water with your ears!

We are discovering that when we slow down, remarkable things happen.

What we have never given a second thought to previously, is now a transformative experience.

We can realise what a miracle the human mind is to be able to conjure up such extraordinary revelations from the ordinary.

We are discovering that when we slow down, remarkable things happen.

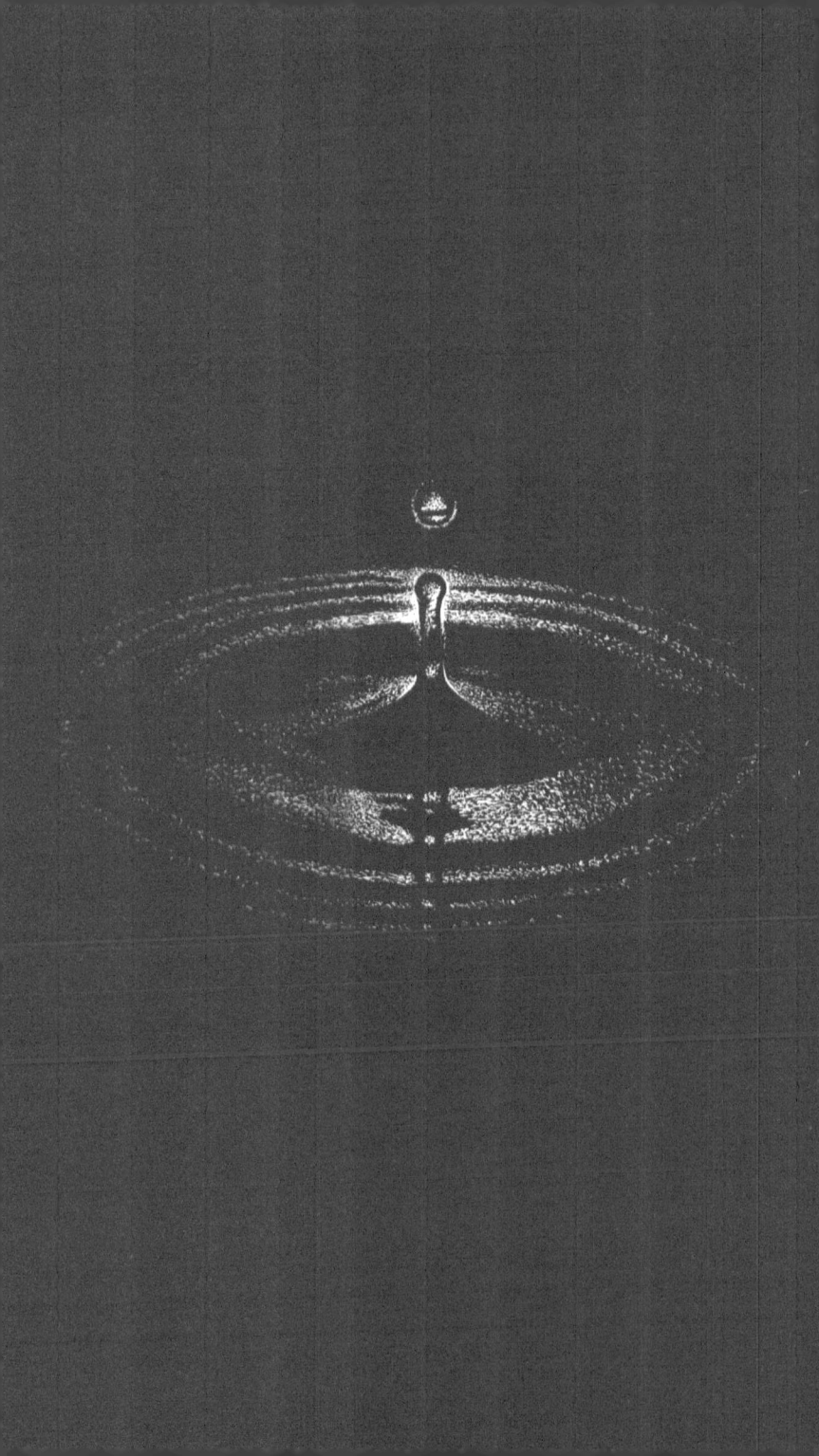

Chapter Nine

The water's endless journey

We have thought about where the water has come from.

But now, where is the water going?

From your mouth, it will move down your throat, and then onwards.

Try and feel it as it moves through your body.

Because this liquid will do more than just satisfy a thirst or cool you.

It will give life to your body, help to hydrate your cells, nourish organs, and flush out toxins.

It can feed your liver, your heart, your lungs, your bones, your blood, your skin, and your hair as it journeys through your intestines on a natural, biological, pre-ordained path.

A journey you don't have to think about.

A pathway developed through billions of years of evolution on this planet.

But what about before it was on this planet? Have you ever thought about that?

What came before the Earth?

How did water first form? How did the planet first form? Where did it all begin?

This water sure does have a story to tell!

You see, taking your time can make you appreciate Everything.

This has a way of relieving the stresses of life. Of simplifying our worries. Of making us realise that our problems, which seems so large when we are caught in them, are really not of great importance to the Universe.

All from the simple act of drinking a glass of water.

And after your body has extracted what it wants from the water, it will continue its journey out of your body.

It may go in to your toilet, be flushed away, never to be thought of again.

But this time can be different.

Because you have made the conscious step to contemplate the amazing path of water.

If you close your eyes, you can imagine the water you have passed now making its way through an underground labyrinth to be joined by the urine of millions of other people that you will never meet or know.

Old people. Young people. People who have monetary wealth. People with spiritual wealth. People experiencing heavy burdens. People who are famous. People who save lives. People who take them. People who birth them. People from all across the spectrum, with their own imperfections and fascinations and stories.

Even the most natural act of going to the toilet, an act we hide from view, is an opportunity for contemplation and beauty.

From all over your city, town, or village, you are now united, far away from your own bodies as what was once inside you is swept out to a sewerage farm, pumped out into yet more tunnels, treated, and repurposed as irrigation on farms to grow food, feed animals, and continue the circle of life.

Ah yes, this everlasting circle of life!

A circle for millions of years to come.

For billions of years. For as long as humans are alive. As we explore other planets. As billions live and die.

This glass of water will take different forms far, far into the future.

This glass of water will take different forms far, far into the future.

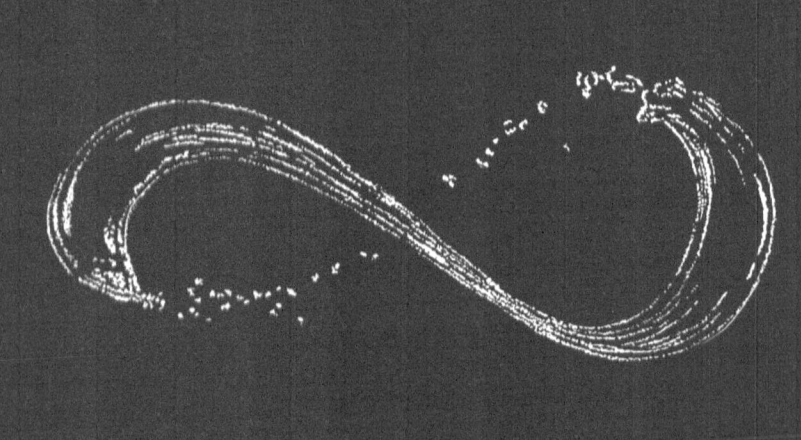

Chapter Ten

Your glass of water is infinite

Who knew that enjoying one glass of water could be so thought-provoking?

Perhaps you read the title of this book, and thought, "How to drink a glass of water? What a silly title for a book. I know how to drink a glass of water!"

That is true. We all know how to do so.

But as you have progressed through drinking your glass of water, you have surely uncovered great depth that you didn't realise was there before.

What takes a few moments (or thirty minutes) is but a short part of the story of water.

Because the water's future it eternal.

It will not always take the form of water.

Its atoms, protons, and neutrons, its building blocks will disassemble, reassemble and metamorphose many times over.

It may become a part of a flower.

It may become part of garbage.

It may become part of a building.

Or a rock.

Perhaps it will form part of a butterfly.

Or a shark.

From its current form as water it will witness the rising and falling of civilisations.

It will be in existence as comets crash into the planet.

As Ice Ages come and go.

As the Sun expands and becomes a Supernova, engulfing and then destroying our home planet.

And then where to for your humble glass of water?

Will it disperse across the infinite expanses of the Universe and become a part of the formation of a new planet?

In what alternate reality will it come to be that someone else, somewhere else in the Universe, will also take the time to enjoy one glass of water in such a way as you are doing?

You see, your choice to spend thirty minutes drinking one glass of water has opened up all sorts of possibilities across infinite time and space.

Chapter Eleven

Finishing your glass of water

As you have drunk your glass of water, you will have considered many things.

Most probably you will have contemplated many things besides what you have read in this book.

The human mind really is special and unique.

Your thoughts are you own, built upon your lifetime of experiences.

Yet, at the same time, we are all together at once, now, in the past, and far into the future.

As you put the glass down, the water that was once inside the glass, not inside of you, think back to what you have just done.

You have been fully present.

You have displayed gratitude.

You have become the glass of water.

The more you practice drinking a glass of water, the more the worries of your world will wash away.

You will drink a glass of water as you drink a glass of water.

You won't think about that work deadline as you drink a glass of water.

You won't worry about mortgage rate rises as you drink a glass of water.

You won't be distracted by social media as you drink a glass of water.

You won't be angry as you drink a glass of water.

You won't be sad as you drink a glass of water.

You won't be stressed as you drink a glass of water.

You will just drink a glass of water.

You can then take these learnings into other parts of your life.

You can learn how to eat an orange.

How to look at a tree.

How to enjoy a painting.

How to walk on a beach.

How to listen to music.

How to breathe.

How to drive a car.

How to listen to a friend.

How to help your family.

Perhaps you may wish to share the experience of drinking a glass of water with your friends, your workmates, and your family?

In this way we can all be together.

We can all be content.

We can all be present.

We can all be alive.

We can all be.

Because when you finish drinking the water, your glass is now empty.

But your cup is full.

About the Author

Alex Wadelton holds the official Guinness world record for the longest duration touching tongue to nose.

He's also danced a marathon in his living room during the world's longest COVID lockdown, plucked his hair out for charity, convinced comedian Tommy Little to become an Instagram model, launched the Big Bash League, won more than a hundred international advertising awards, helped convince Australian supermarkets to stop their short-term plastic promotions, got a statue made of the iconic stance against racism by Nicky Winmar with the AFL, won "The Pitch" on ABCTV's Gruen, appeared on Channel Ten's The Project five times, raised over a million dollars for charity in his spare time, been described as "one of the world's best-paid advertising engineers" on a Hungarian website, been labelled "an obvious nut job liberal" on the front page of The Daily Mirror UK website, and co-authored two best-selling books with creative visionary Russel Howcroft titled The Right Brain Workout Volumes 1 & 2.

All because of his consistent use of the 'c' word: creativity.

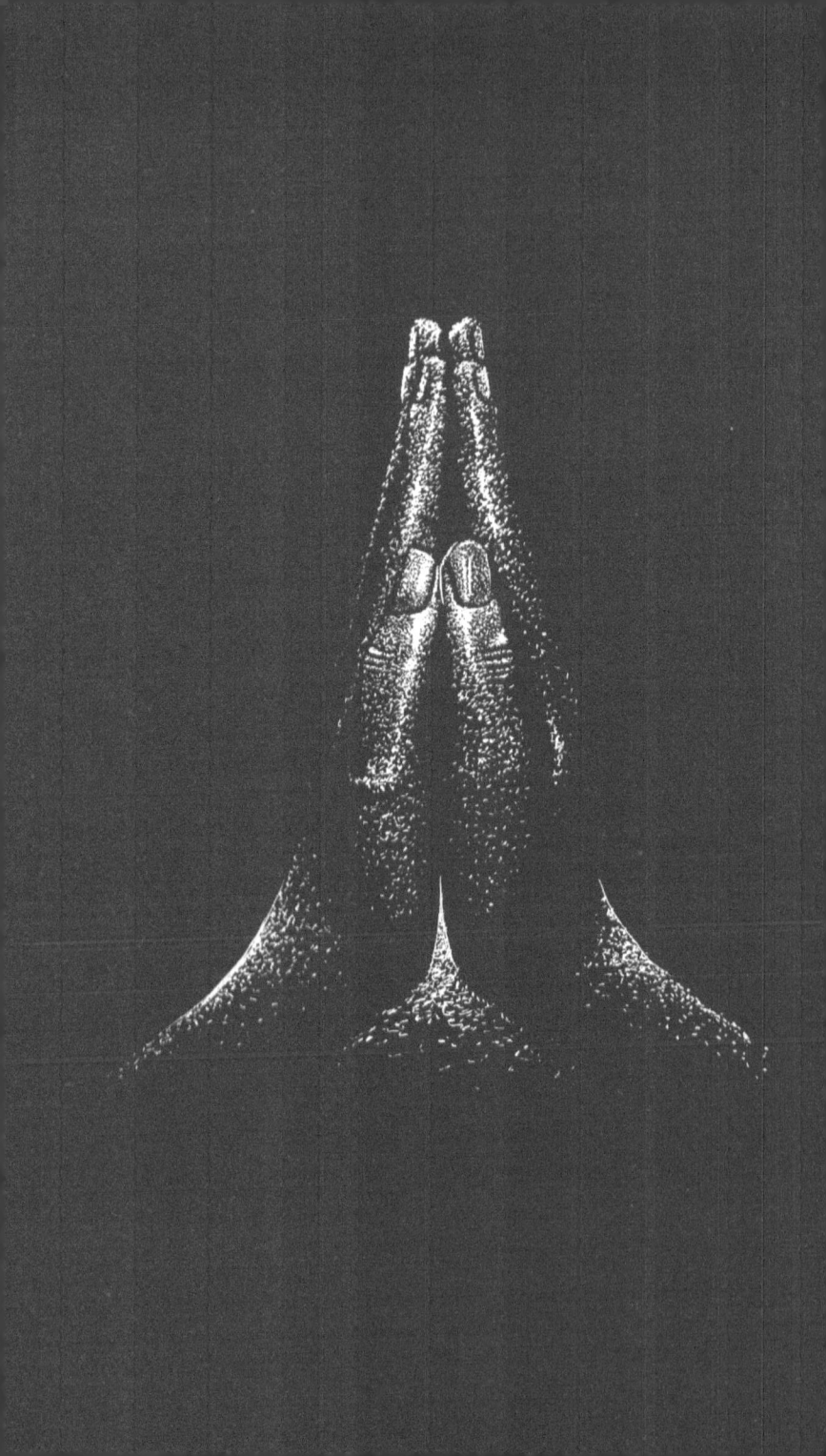

Acknowledgments

The journey to find magic in a glass of water would have been much more difficult without the guidance and support of my wonderful wife Sheridan. Thank you for everything.

To my beautiful children Roarke and Lila, thank you for being you. I learn so much from you every day.

Let us all drink in life together, forever.

www.ingramcontent.com/pod-product-compliance
Lightning Source LLC
Chambersburg PA
CBHW020330010526
44107CB00054B/2058